ADHD KIDS & PARENTAL CONTROL
The Ultimate truth behind effective parenting and kid control

Adam Hills

Table of contents

Chapter 1

The truth about kids with ADHD

What is ADHD

It's common for youngsters to periodically forget their homework, daydream during class, behave without thinking, or grow fidgety at the dinner table. But inattention, impulsivity, and hyperactivity are also indications of attention deficit hyperactivity disorder (ADHD), also known as attention deficit disorder or ADD.

ADHD is a common neurodevelopmental disease that often presents in early infancy, usually before the age of seven. ADHD makes it difficult for youngsters to suppress their spontaneous responses—responses that might entail anything from movement to speech to concentration. We all know kids who can't sit still, who never seem to listen, who don't follow directions no matter how precisely you explain them, or who blurt out inappropriate statements at unsuitable moments. Sometimes these youngsters are regarded as troublemakers, or scolded for being indolent and undisciplined. However, they may have ADHD.

Is it typical child behavior or is it ADHD?

It might be difficult to discern between ADHD and regular "kid behavior." If you see only a few signals, or the symptoms present only in particular scenarios, it's probably not ADHD. On the other hand, if your child shows many ADHD signs and symptoms that are present across all situations—at home, at school, and at play—it's time to take a closer look.

Life with a child with ADHD can be frustrating and overwhelming, but as a parent, there is a lot you can do to help control symptoms, overcome daily challenges, and bring greater calm to your family.

Myths and Facts about ADHD

Myth: All kids with ADHD are hyperactive.

Fact: Some children with ADHD are hyperactive, but many others with concentration issues are not. Children with ADHD who are inattentive, but not overly active, may appear to be spacey and unmotivated.

ADHD symptoms

When many people think of attention deficit disorder, they imagine an out-of-control youngster in continuous activity, bouncing off the walls and upsetting everyone around. But the reality is much more complex. Some children with ADHD are hyperactive, while others sit quietly—with their attention miles away. Some put too much focus on a task and have trouble shifting it to something else. Others are just moderately inattentive, yet highly impulsive.

Children with ADHD may be Inattentive, yet neither hyperactive nor impulsive.

Hyperactive and impulsive, yet able to pay attention.

Inattentive, hyperactive, and impulsive (the most common form of ADHD).

Children who just have inattentive signs of ADHD are typically disregarded because they're not disruptive. However, the signs of inattention have consequences.

Getting in hot water with parents and instructors for not following orders, underperforming in school, or arguing with other kids for not playing by the rules.

Because we anticipate very young children to be readily distractible and energetic, it's the impulsive behaviors, the risky climb, the blurted insult, that typically stick out in preschoolers with ADHD. By age four or five, though, most children have learned how to pay attention to others, to sit quietly when instructed to, and not to say everything that pops into their heads. So by the time children reach school age, people with ADHD stand out in all three behaviors: inattentiveness, hyperactivity, and impulsivity.

Inattentiveness indications and symptoms of ADHD

It isn't that children with ADHD can't pay attention,

when they're doing activities they love or hearing about issues in which they're engaged, they have no problem concentrating and staying on target. But when the work is repetitious or dull, they soon tune out.

Staying on track is another major challenge. Children with ADHD sometimes jump from activity to task without finishing any of them or miss key stages in processes. Organizing their academics and their time is tougher for them than it is for other youngsters. Kids with ADHD also have problems focusing if there are activities going on around them; they normally require a calm, quiet atmosphere to remain focused.

Symptoms of inattention in children

Your youngster may:

Have problems keeping concentrated; be quickly sidetracked or grow bored with a job before it's done.

Appear not to listen when talked to.

Have trouble remembering things and following directions; do not pay attention to details or makes thoughtless blunders.

Have problems remaining organized, planning, and completing jobs.

Frequently lose or misplace schoolwork, books, toys, or other stuff.

Hyperactivity signs and symptoms of ADHD

The most evident indicator of ADHD is hyperactivity. While many youngsters are naturally highly active, kids with hyperactive signs of attention deficit disorder are continually moving. They may attempt to accomplish numerous things at once, jumping about from one task to the next. Even when forced to remain motionless, which may be extremely difficult for them, their foot is tapping, their leg is trembling, or their fingers are drumming.

Symptoms of hyperactivity in children

Your youngster may:

Constantly fidget and wriggle.

Have trouble sitting still, playing quietly, or relaxing.

Move around continuously, often sprinting or climbing illegally.

Talk excessively.

Have a quick temper or "short fuse."

Impulsive indications and symptoms of ADHD

The impulsivity of children with ADHD might create difficulty with self-control. Because they restrain themselves less than other kids do, they'll interrupt talks, violate other people's space, ask irrelevant questions in class, make tactless remarks, and ask too intimate inquiries. Instructions like, "Be patient" and "Just wait a little while" are twice as hard for children with ADHD to obey as they are for other kids.

Children with impulsive indications and symptoms of ADHD also tend to be temperamental and to overreact emotionally. As a consequence, people may start to see the youngster as rude, odd, or needy.

Symptoms of impulsivity in children

Your youngster may:

Act without thinking.

Guess, rather than spending time to solve a problem; blurt out answers in class without waiting to be called on or hear the complete question.

Intrude in other people's discussions or games.

Often interrupt people; speak the incorrect thing at the wrong moment.

Be unable to keep overwhelming emotions under control, resulting in furious outbursts or temper tantrums.

Positive impacts of ADHD on children

ADHD has nothing to do with IQ or skill. What's more, youngsters with attention deficit disorder typically display the following beneficial traits:

Creativity. Children who have ADHD may be extraordinarily creative and inventive. The youngster who daydreams and has 10 separate thoughts at once might become a brilliant problem-solver, a wellspring of ideas, or an innovative artist. Children with ADHD may be easily distracted, yet occasionally they see what others don't see.

Flexibility. Because children with ADHD explore a variety of possibilities at once, they don't get fixed on one solution early on and are more receptive to other ideas.

Enthusiasm and spontaneity. Children with ADHD are seldom boring! They're interested in a lot of different areas and have dynamic personalities. In sum, if they're not annoying you (and sometimes even when they are), they're a lot of fun to be around.

Energy and drive. When youngsters with ADHD are motivated, they work or play hard and seek to achieve. It truly may be tough to divert kids from a work that fascinates them, particularly if the activity is participatory or hands-on.

Is it actually ADHD?

Just because a kid displays signs of inattention, impulsivity, or hyperactivity does not guarantee that they have ADHD. Certain medical diseases, psychiatric problems, and stressful life experiences might generate symptoms that appear like ADHD.

Before an accurate diagnosis of ADHD can be established, you must consult a mental health expert to examine and rule out the following possibilities:

Learning difficulties or challenges with reading, writing, motor skills, or language.

Major life events or painful experiences, such as a recent relocation, loss of a loved one, bullying, or divorce.

Psychological problems include anxiety, sadness, or bipolar illness.

Behavioral disorders such as conduct disorder, reactive

attachment disorder, and oppositional defiant disorder. Medical diseases, including thyroid difficulties, neurological ailments, epilepsy, and sleep disturbances.

Whether or whether your child's symptoms of inattention, hyperactivity, and impulsivity are related to ADHD, they may create numerous difficulties if left untreated. Children who can't concentrate and control themselves may struggle in school, get into regular problems, and find it hard to get along with others or make friends. These disappointments and problems may lead to poor self-esteem as well as friction and stress for the entire family.

But therapy may make a huge impact on your child's symptoms. With the correct help, your kid may get on track for success in all aspects of life.

If your kid suffers from symptoms that seem like

ADHD, don't delay to seek expert treatment. You may manage your child's symptoms of hyperactivity, inattention, and impulsivity without obtaining a diagnosis of attention deficit disorder. Options to start with include enrolling your kid into counseling, following a healthy diet and exercise plan, and altering the home environment to avoid distractions.

If you do obtain a diagnosis of ADHD, you may then work with your child's doctor, therapist, and school to establish a tailored treatment plan that suits their requirements. Effective treatment for childhood ADHD requires behavioral therapy, parent education and training, social support, and aid at school. Medication may also be utilized; however, it should never be the main attention deficit disorder therapy.

While attention deficit disorder is not caused by inadequate parenting, there are effective parenting practices that may go a long way to fix troublesome behaviors. Children with ADHD need structure, consistency, clear communication, and rewards and consequences for their behavior. They also need lots of love, support, and encouragement.

There are many things parents can do to reduce the signs and symptoms of ADHD without sacrificing the natural energy, playfulness, and sense of wonder unique in every child.

Take care of yourself so you're better equipped to care for your kid. Eat healthy, exercise, get enough sleep, find methods to minimize stress, and seek face-to-face support from family and friends as well as your child's doctor and teachers.

Establish structure and keep to it. Help your kid remain focused and organized by following daily routines, streamlining your child's schedule, and keeping your youngster engaged with healthful activities.

Set clear expectations. Make the rules of conduct straightforward and explain what will happen when they are followed or broken—and follow through each time with a reward or a punishment.

Encourage activity and sleep. Physical exercise increases focus and support brain development. Importantly for children with ADHD, it also leads to improved sleep, which in turn helps alleviate the symptoms of ADHD

Chapter 2

How to know when you are triggered by your kids

Have you ever experienced that feeling? That flush of rage when your kid is misbehaving? Whether it's tossing food away or just refusing to answer questions, kids have various ways of getting on our nerves and are always pushing our limits.

We hear a great lot about the significance of emotional self-regulation in youngsters. Sure, you need to teach your kid how to handle emotions, but without a clear and constant awareness of your feelings, your child's emotional health may be left to chance.

I've listened to parents rant on and on about kids who disregard basic directions, quarrel with siblings or, throw the rare temper tantrums when they don't get what they want.

"I feel furious when my kid compares me to his closest friend's mom," laments Maria, a parent in one of our parenting group sessions. It's disheartening that an 8-year-old can draw such parallels.

Although your kids might drive you up a wall with their words and behaviors, you must strive for balance and self-regulation. You may be prone to an overreaction, feeling justified that your child's actions led to your response. It all occurs in a rush, and you may be tempted to make a wishy-washy resolve. Before you know it, you notice your kids showing the same types of overreactions that appear unconnected to the conditions that provoked them.

Before it is too late, you must develop cognizance of your emotional responses. You must recognize that your youngsters are fragile and inexperienced. Are you overreacting to the things kids do?

Let the question above linger in your head for a time.

Is it conceivable that your child's actions may have reminded you of anything from your past?

Some parents report that their outbursts at their children weren't at all meant, that it seemed like they were not able to control themselves. Suppose you've discovered yourself in a group of persons who excessively overreact. In that case, I have news for you, if you don't quit at the first opportunity you have, you will successfully establish a cycle of unresolved feelings.

This post will teach you practical strategies that can help you recognize your emotional triggers and control them. After all, you want your children to control and regulate their emotions; You should be certain that you're not standing in their way.

Understanding Emotional\Experts concur that unresolved trauma may travel through generations and continue to affect youngsters for a long time. When you become aware of your triggers, you raise the chances to favor a good reaction for your child's emotional wellness. Suppose there are already certain instances where your unconscious, unreasonable behaviors are affecting your kid. In such an instance, you may then start taking serious actions to remedy those difficulties. Most times, all you need to do is take a step back and examine a scenario. It is only through identifying your triggers that you would be able to react more proactively.

If you identify your emotional triggers, you will unearth the foundations of your prior emotional scars that affect the way you connect with your kid. With this insight, you will create a caring atmosphere for your kid.

Chapter 3

Being a compassionate parent

Here's the good news. There's no such thing as a perfect parent. In actuality, being (or appearing) "perfect" isn't beneficial. We're not making it up — science says so, and it's not even new news! In the 1950s, pediatrician Dr. Donald Winnicott developed the notion that the 'good enough' parent was, in fact, better than the ideal parent. So, let's look at how to be a good parent.

Firstly, what do kids genuinely need? A recent analysis of children's views on their well-being and happiness showed that "Feeling loved and having positive, supportive relationships, particularly with friends and family, including having someone to talk to and rely on were consistently stated as a top priority for children to have a happy life."

Perhaps you had the world's best parents, or perhaps there are things you'd like to do differently.

If you're continuously exploring books on parental control and guidance, then start by employing your upbringing as a resource.

This could be challenging but self-reflection and awareness are vital to straightening out those parenting knots, especially when you find yourself reacting emotionally to something your child achieves or fails to do. When this happens, ask yourself why. For example, if you discover that you feel irritated and impatient with your child asking you to lead them through their maths homework every week, take a moment to review how your parents helped you (or didn't) with schooling and how that impacted you.

It's hard to offer a whole list of desired parenting qualities, but here are a few that often come out on top!

Be positive

One of the top qualities of good parents is positivity. Praising kids doesn't spoil them, and complimenting them on behavior and achievements only encourages more of the same while building self-esteem. Think about how you respond to favorable comments from your employer or a lover.

If your kid comes to you with a problem, work through it together. A smart parenting technique is to start by identifying answers together rather than solving issues for them. This will help your kid build the abilities they need to navigate through future obstacles more independently. By contrast, negative input like criticizing or expressing things like 'why can't you be more like X' does not help in any way.

Communicate

As they say "All behavior is communication." Whether your toddler is upset because you gave them a blue spoon (and they were looking forward to choosing the green one – one of the few choices they're allowed to make in a day) or your teenager is starting arguments at the dinner table (because they're learning to think critically and challenge things – an important and valuable skill), what your kids do and say is the best evidence you have for what's going on in their minds and worlds.

If your child tells you that they're unhappy, it doesn't imply you've failed at being a parent, but merely that they need your assistance in managing their emotions. Let them know that you're listening to them by acknowledging their discontent and letting them say it rather than racing to replies.

The technique in which we talk to our kids is vital. Just because youngsters lack life experience, it doesn't entail we should talk down to them. Sometimes, it's simpler for us to scream comments from up high than to explain what's going on. Remember, even tiny kids can understand explanations better than you realize.

Your child says: I don't want to wear my seat belt! It hurts!

You say: You have to wear your seat belt!

Try saying: I understand it could be uncomfortable occasionally but I want you to be as safe as possible while we're in the car - your safety is crucial to me.

Just as the greatest leaders recognize their weaknesses,

the best parents confess when they've made a mistake. If you get something wrong or lose your rage unnecessarily, don't be scared to address it and apologies. This shows your youngsters that adults screw up too. Again, being immaculate helps no one.

Be their safe refuge

You cannot ruin a kid by showing them too much affection. Hugs and affirmations of love should be as plentiful as your child needs them to be. Showing unconditional love, even when there's been a difficulty or an upset will help your youngster feel more protected.

If they damage themselves, display concern rather than attempting to brush off their pain or suffering. This won't lead to their using you for comfort or sympathy, and if you discover that they do, it's wiser to find out why than than denying them their haven.

Responding to what your youngster is saying to you verbally, physically, and emotionally is vital to their development. In actuality, studies have found that "Children, especially preterm children, displayed speedier cognitive gain when mothers were consistently responsive."

In social circumstances, it may be easy to be waylaid by other people's expectations. Don't force interactions on your child, especially physical ones. Laying down the boundaries of consent and control over their bodies could be a frightening one to think about but simple to implement if you talk about it honestly.

Whether you give your youngster the mantra of "my body, my choice" or allow them to select whether to say goodbye to people with a hug, a high five, or a wave – helping them to determine how they interact with others is crucial.

Be consistent

Kids demand boundaries and consistency. You'll need to think about punishment at some point – but remember that the aim is to help them discover their way to behavior that isn't destructive to others and learn to regulate their own emotions. Physical discipline such as spanking doesn't work. According to Katie McLaughlin, a clinical psychologist and Harvard professor; "We know that spanking is not healthy and may be detrimental to children's development and elevates the chance of mental health issues."

Rules and routines assist children to know what's expected of them and what's coming next. Involving older kids in the creation of rules and routines could prevent them from feeling things are being pushed on them unfairly.

Having restrictions in place doesn't mean you can't be flexible, especially as your kids mature. What was an appropriate rule for a toddler that may be less suitable for a little child? Watching their restrictions rise urges children towards greater independence.

Give them your time

For busy working parents, it's common to want to treat your kids to larger, more costly, activities to make up for the times when you haven't been there. Whether you work because you need to, or you work because you like your job - or a combination of the two- you do not need to feel guilty for working.

Think of it like this, how can we encourage our kids to work hard to get into careers that they love if they're then expected to give them up when they have their kids? What does that teach them?

What is crucial is quality time. If, like most fantastic parents, you're time-poor and nervous that you aren't spending enough quality time with your kid - try introducing a play session where they pick what you do. Give them half an hour (or as long you can spend) where you actively engage in their favorite activity and do nothing else in that time no laundry, no phones, no distractions. You may learn that it turns out to be their favorite time of the day.

Self-Care (and self-kindness)

You are your child's first role model so if they don't see you taking care of yourself, how will they learn how to do the same for themselves?

A recent survey found that 88% of women aged 35-49 who care for kids and their elderly parents felt concerned at work. That's hardly unexpected considering the plethora of chores each parent has to perform. Parenting can be hard and there are days when you drop in a tired heap onto the sofa after loading the dishwasher, clearing away the toys, and making tomorrow's lunch - and then you hear a howl from upstairs and want to burst into tears yourself.

The greatest parents know how to ask for aid. If you have a partner, be sure you're sharing the responsibility in a way that works for you — and if you're not, take action to remedy it. Find techniques to offer each other time off. For some, this works ad hoc but for others, knowing you have a lie-in to look forward to on a particular day could help.

For couples, setting in time to reconnect after a hard week of kid-wrangling and working is usually disregarded. Use your support network and organize friends to babysit so that you may leave the house and go for dinner together.

If you can afford it, outsource the duties you dislike so you may prioritize family time and time alone. Do not, under any circumstances, compare oneself to others, especially on social media. If you encounter a picture-perfect family online, realize that it's only a snapshot, not a continuous reality.

The fact that you're reading this post suggests you're a good parent.

That said, being a good parent doesn't have to mean studying every parenting manual under the sun. It's more about taking time to communicate, reflect and adapt. No one gets it right all the time so don't beat yourself up when you get it wrong.

Chapter 4

Listening to your kids

Listening, as it is, is a tough thing. And to think of listening to your kid is a huge endeavor. Is it vital to listen to your child? Add to that the reality that when the youngster wants to be listened to, you may have another 1000 things racing on your mind urging you to simply leap off your seat right now.

However, a study says that listening to your kids makes it more likely that they listen to you (which most of us want). When a youngster feels listened to, he is more inclined to listen, and having been understood, he will grasp your point of view too. It helps parents and children create better links and relationships, and increases their self-esteem.

Without you being even aware of it, your day-to-day conduct impacts your kid in numerous ways, defining his or her future personality. As parents, you affect your child's life purposefully or unwittingly, or both.

From the tone of your voice to the words you pick, your kid learns the skills required to engage with you - as parents are a child's first instructor. Children who are not heard become the ones who never listen. They will constantly be under the assumption that they are undeserving of your time and attention.

Whatever they do, think, or feel is bad. They lose confidence and self-esteem, which may be damaging to their development as young adults. A youngster who is regularly evaluated or chastised lacks interest in sharing and connecting and ends up being isolated, alone, and distant.

Some kids are naturally vocal, and they talk everything out, while others may require a lot of encouragement to be able to communicate with you. The first approach is to be open to hearing and offer your youngster your full attention. When you listen to your kid, you get to know what they are thinking, experiencing, and going through. Childhood is a challenging time, and with little speech, children frequently find it difficult to explain their emotions.

Children must be heard so that they do not bottle up their emotions. It also implies that your children will listen to you more since they have been heard. This offers up doors for constructive talks, which are beneficial and bring parents and children closer.

As you can see, a strong emotional reaction may have long-term implications for both you and your kid. So, it is crucial for you as a parent to understand and better regulate your feelings and responses. In reality, being self-aware is a vital skill in good parenting; learning to self-regulate your emotions is as important.

But how can you achieve this daily? Here are a few basic practical strategies to be more in touch with your emotions and of course, control them better.

Chapter 5

Handling your emotion.

Parenting can be a profoundly emotional process. Daily, you may be dealing with an angry toddler, an aggressive primary schooler, or, a resentful teenager. Added to this, you frequently have to cope with pressures at work and in your everyday life. So certainly, parenthood can be extremely tough. It might create intense sensations in you that can be difficult to handle.

Even if your anger is not aimed at your kid, your furious responses might affect her feelings and consequently, her conduct. For example, when your kid hears an argument or a fight between you and your spouse, or between family members, she feels what is termed 'background rage'. This may harm her emotionally and socially as she grows older.

Research has repeatedly established that a parent's emotional reaction directly affects a child's emotional response and conduct. Suppose your child wants to wear a green hair clip but you want her to wear matching yellow hair clips. She is already on the edge of a breakdown. In this case, if you reply with impatience and frustration, you would just add to her suffering. On the other hand, if you sympathize with her and say, "I realize that you want to wear the green clip today. Would you want to try on both green and yellow clips to determine which one looks best with your outfit today?" Your youngster will probably reply more calmly. The key here is how you respond and react to a certain event. That is why it is equally vital to study and investigate how your emotional reactions might affect both you and your kid.